February!

Happy

Daniel!

Love,
Gaga

February 2, 2015
Happy Birthday,
Daniel!

Love,
Gaga

**T is for T.rex**
**Some of God's Most Amazing Creatures from A to Z**

First printing: 2013

Clouds of Light Publications, LLC
P.O. Box 1835
Castle Rock, CO 80104
www.cloudsoflightpublications.com

ISBN 10: 0988281252
ISBN 13: 978-0-9882812-5-7

Authored by Terry P. Beh
Illustrations by Daniel W. Sorensen; The Art of Daniel W. Sorensen, http://www.dansorensen.com

Printed in the United States of America by Bookmasters, Inc., 30 Amberwood Parkway, Ashland, OH 44805.
Job #M10131, January 2013.

All Scripture quotes in this book are taken from the New King James Version of the Bible.

For additional information and features related to this book, please visit www.tisfortrex.com.

**Library of Congress Control Number: 201290330**

Beh, Terry P.
T is for t.rex: some of god's most amazing creatures from a to z / written by T.P. Beh; illustrated by Daniel W. Sorensen
p. cm.
Includes index
ISBN 13: 978-0-9882812-5-7

2012920330

# T is for T.rex

## Some of God's Most Amazing Creatures from A to Z

Written by T.P. Beh
Illustrated by Daniel W. Sorensen

Clouds of Light Publications, LLC

## Acknowledgements

*I owe many people a great deal of thanks for the publication of this book. First, I'd like to thank my illustrator Dan Sorensen for his fantastic gifts of imagination and creativity that have brought this book to life and made it something people might actually want to pick up and read. Known as "Dan the dragon man," Dan is not only a first-rate artist but a fellow believer, which made working with him easy—despite my sometimes maddening instructions.*

*I would also like to thank the friends and fellow creationists who prayed for or contributed to this book in one way or another. Many thanks to my Wednesday morning guys and Sunday School class for their encouragement and prayers. Particular thanks to Joe Taylor, Otis Kline, Brian Thomas, Doug & Donna Barker, and my kids, Christian & Amanda, for reviewing the manuscript and giving me their honest and helpful feedback (not always good!), and to Pastor Craig Smith for his kind technical assistance. Special thanks to Dr. Gary Parker for giving so generously of his time to thoroughly examine T is for T.rex from a creation science perspective and for his invaluable input!*

*Undying thanks to Ken Maupin for his wise personal and professional advice and counsel—it is no exaggeration to say that without Ken this book would have never gotten off the ground! Much love and appreciation to my wife Anne, who graciously supported my desire to work full-time on this book and to spend inheritance money on getting it published. And deep gratitude to my mother Mary Beh, whose gift from heaven made the whole thing possible.*

*Finally, everlasting thanks to God, our Father, and our Lord Jesus Christ, by Whose mercy and grace all things are possible, and Who, in Their great wisdom and power, created all things—including the dinosaurs and the other strange and wonderful creatures mentioned in this book.*

**—Terry P. Beh**

*There are so many people I want to thank. First to my mother Janet, father William (Dad, I wish you could be here to see it), sister Tracy and brother Dean, who always believed in me, encouraged me to do what I loved and never stopped asking me about my art.*

*It's all a journey to me. You meet people who come and go and add to your life. You also meet people who are consistent companions in your journey. And there are friends who may no longer be part of your life, but when you talk to or see them again it's like they've always been there.*

*So, thank you Ken, Jeremy, Kim, Lance, Holly, Sean, my Ohioan friends, Steve and Sue, Jeff, Dan, everyone I've met at the Glen Workshop, Lisa, Heather, my fellow ASOTians and so many others who I know I haven't mentioned (forgive me). All of you believed in me when I didn't always see it in myself, and I needed that. And, when I finally started down the right road, you were there cheering me on.*

*But there's one Person behind it all Who orchestrates my life, and, as Terry (thank you, as well) mentioned above, I give full credit to Jesus Christ. It's pretty cool that I get to be a creator like my Father in heaven. To be able to create that which never existed before is quite the gift He has given me! Thank you, Lord.*

**—Daniel W. Sorensen**

# Introduction

Do you love dinosaurs like I do? I'm guessing that if you're reading this book the answer is a big "yes"! Dinosaurs are amazing creatures, and it's a lot of fun to think about how they might have looked and lived, as well as what happened to them. The size some of them reached, their odd "reptilian" appearance and the large horns, claws, teeth and other strange features fascinate us and appeal to our imaginations.

Because dinosaurs are generally thought to be extinct and little is known about their behavior, they make for great characters in fictional movies, books, TV programs, comic books, magazines, etc. Unfortunately, much of what we "know" (or think we know) about these "terrible lizards" is based more on Hollywood and popular imagination than on scientific facts—even the images we have of them are largely based on artistic interpretation. For everything we know about them comes from fossil evidence, like footprints, coprolite (fossilized poop) and bones. (In recent years even some fossilized dinosaur skin and organs have been found!) However, while fossil evidence like this can give us clues about how dinosaurs walked, what they ate and how they looked, it is limited in what it can tell us, especially about things like their coloration and how they behaved.

For, while fossilized dinosaur bones exist in the present, and though scientists can study them and perform repeatable tests on them to come up with objective, testable results, as far as we currently know, dinosaur *behavior* existed only in the past. And scientists are no better at answering questions about the past than are lawyers and historians—or novelists and filmmakers (whose stories are judged more by their popularity than by their truthfulness). For instance, while we know from their fossils that *T.rex* had large claws and sharp teeth, how can we be sure how they were used? Most people, including evolutionists, assume that large teeth and sharp claws mean the animal was a meat eater. However, scientists know of many animals with sharp teeth and claws today that are just vegetarians, so scientists cannot objectively determine T.rex's diet because they have never observed *T.rex* behavior.

If only we had a record of what happened back when *T.rex* was around written by a reliable witness, then we could know how dinosaurs behaved. Well, it turns out that we do! The Bible is just such a record of earth's history written by the only One to witness it from the beginning: God Himself. And the Bible tells us that God originally created all animals to eat plants (GENESIS 1:29-30). It also tells us that Sin brought death and struggle into God's original, perfect Creation, and that some animals (and people) thereafter began to kill others (GEN. 3-4). Today, some animals with big claws and sharp teeth, like panda bears, still reflect their original creation and eat only plants, while others, like tigers, reflect the Corruption of our world that took place following Sin and now eat meat. Even the diet of that ferocious "predator," the grizzly bear, is about 80%-90% plants! So, when it comes to *T.rex* claws and teeth, what we can be sure of is that they were originally used to gather and chew vegetation. As creation scientist Dr. Gary Parker likes to say, "What we see in God's world agrees with what we read in God's Word."

Apart from finding solid fossil evidence—like *Tyrannosaurus rex* teeth embedded in the bone of another dinosaur (and there is such evidence)—we can only speculate that they became meat eaters. And while skeletons, even nearly complete ones, can give us a general idea of what dinosaurs looked like, no one knows exactly how they appeared or how they acted. Therefore, while all illustrations based on fossils involve some "artistic license," we have sought to represent the animals in this book as accurately as possible based on biblical and scientific facts.

# T is for T.rex
## Some of God's Most Amazing Creatures from A to Z

### CONTENTS

# A is for ALLOSAURUS

The Allosaurus was, of core-us,
a dinosaur that looks carnivorous.
In the Garden of Eden, which God made all good,
plants and not us would have been his food.
We could have lived with dinos 'til Sin changed what we eat,
and some animals, perhaps like allosaurs, began to eat meat.
Then, with its big claws and sharp, knife-like teeth,
an Allosaurus could prob'ly have eaten three or four of us!

**Allosaurus** (AL-uh-SORE-us, "Different Lizard") was bi-pedal (walked on two legs), had two short horns above its eyes, could reach 35 feet in length, stand up to 17 feet tall, weigh over two tons, and had sharp teeth and three large claws on each foot and hand. Allosaurs are usually pictured as predators, and perhaps even hunted in packs like wolves. Their fossils are primarily found in the western United States—one mass *Allosaurus* gravesite in Utah has produced bones from over 40 individuals from juveniles to adults! This strongly suggests that they were killed, buried and fossilized by a great catastrophe, such as Noah's flood in the Bible (GENESIS 6-9), and not by any normal processes operating in nature today—a great example of the truth that God's Word is the surest guide to understanding God's world. And since the Bible also says that all land animals were created on the 6th day of creation, before the Flood allosaurs also co-existed on earth with men, though hopefully not too closely!

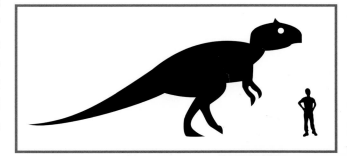

# B is for BRONTOSAURUS

The Brontosaur is no more—
now they're called Apatosaurus.
"How apt is that?" one may implore
(I still prefer to call them "Bronto").
But, as some say, "Don't be a boor,
and learn 'Apato' pronto!"
Then again, you might agree with
the book of Job, where they're called "behemoth."

**Brontosaurus** (BRON-tuh-SORE-us, "Thunder Lizard")—now renamed **Apatosaurus** (ah-PAT-uh-SORE-us, "Deceptive Lizard"), because its discoverer had put the wrong head and body together, was one of the largest creatures that ever lived. A plant-eating sauropod with a long neck and tail and a huge body, it could be 70 to 90 feet long and weigh over 30 tons. It had elephant-like feet that could be nearly a yard wide! In the biblical book of Job, God describes a creature called "behemoth" that sounds a lot like an apatosaur/brontosaur: it "eats grass," its "strength is in his hips," "his power is in his stomach muscles," it "moves his tail like a cedar (tree)" and has "bones…like beams of bronze," JOB 40:15-24. While some think God was talking about an elephant or a hippo, the Middle Eastern cedar tree is one of the largest trees in the world, something like a redwood, so this animal clearly had a large and powerful tail—exactly like a sauropod dinosaur. And since the Lord was clearly describing an animal Job was familiar with, it had to have been alive just a few thousand years ago!

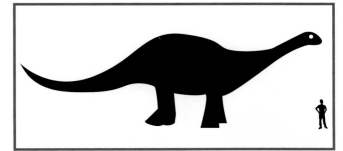

# C is for CEOLOPHYSIS

The Ceolophysis, in a crisis,
could run so fast (like maybe thrice us)
that in a race they'd slice and dice us!
Nonetheless, without distinction,
Ceolos failed to outrun mass extinction
(which wasn't caused by evolution).
Down in old New Mexico,
they died by scores in Noah's mighty flow.

**Ceolophysis** (SEE-low-FIE-sis, "Hollow Form") was a relatively small, bi-pedal dinosaur about nine feet long and three feet high, which is thought to have been a meat eater. Its name comes from the fact that its limb bones were hollow. Nimble and lightweight, it was probably a fast runner and may have lived in groups. Hundreds of well-preserved *Ceolophysis* skeletons have been found buried together in a "mass grave" at Ghost Ranch, New Mexico. This indicates that, like the mass allosaur gravesite in Utah, they were the victims of a massive, catastrophic event, such as the worldwide flood of Noah that killed them all at the same time and buried them together in a common grave. In fact, there are many such large "bone yards" around the world, often containing the fossils of many different plants and animals from widely different environments, which shows they weren't formed by local floods.

# D is for DIMETRODON

Dimetrodon was, in times bye gone,
a fierce and toothy creature—
a big, tall frill upon its back was its most distinctive feature.
As it walked along the swamp, its sail it could turn
to soak up sun and warm itself or to avoid a burn.
Called by some a "proto-mammal,"
there's no proof Dimetrodon evolved into a camel.

**Dimetrodon** (die-ME-tro-DON, "Two Measures of Teeth"), a so-called "mammal-like reptile," was not a dinosaur, but a pelycosaur, a group that is poorly defined by science. It was named for its two kinds of teeth: shearing teeth and canine teeth. A big, swamp-dwelling creature with a tall sail or frill on its back, *Dimetrodon* grew to 11 feet long and over 500 pounds. With its large head and sharp teeth, it could have become a fierce predator in a sin-cursed world. While said to be closer to mammals than reptiles, it was cold-blooded like a lizard (probably using its sail to regulate its body temperature), had four legs that stuck out from the sides of its body like a lizard, and walked and ran just like a lizard! In short, as the Bible says, it was a distinctive "kind" and could only reproduce other dimetrodons (GEN. 1). Bones of this animal are primarily found in the Permian "red beds" of Texas and Oklahoma.

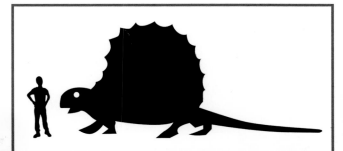

# E is for ERYOPS

That Eryops sure had some chops!—
but not like a musician.
At five-feet long it couldn't sing a song,
but was a big, ol', green amphibian!
It prob'ly ate those giant dragonflies
that flew around ancient swamps,
or rolled them up, sorta donut-like,
to sell to Permian cops!

"Permian" isn't something girls do to their hair, but an early sediment layer. Evolutionists believe it represents a time 250-300 million years ago. Creationists think it was deposited by Noah's flood only about 4,500 years in the past.

**Eryops** (EAR-ee-OPS, "Drawn-out Face") was a large, salamander-like amphibian that could be five feet long and weigh 200 pounds! It had a broad, flat head and short, sturdy limbs. It lived in the same environment as *Dimetrodon*, but, like a salamander, dwelt partly on land and partly in the water. With nostrils on the top of its head, *Eryops* may have been a stealth hunter like a crocodile, floating just beneath the surface of the water with just its eyes and nostrils showing as it snuck up on its prey. While evolution says that amphibians like *Eryops* evolved into reptiles, the Bible says that God made all the animal "kinds" during the first week of creation (GEN. 1:21-25) and that they remain that way (an amphibian remains an amphibian). Along with *Dimetrodon*, *Eryops* bones are also found in the Permian "red beds" of Texas.

# F is for FLYING REPTILES

Flying reptiles could soar for miles and miles,
like leather-winged projectiles, searching for a fish pie.
Yes, they searched for fish near the top of the sea,
then swooped and scooped them hastily.
With strange names like Quetzalcoatlus,
they might look like a heck of a bat to us!
Some even say that they might still be around,
though it won't be a fact until they are found.

Known as **Pterosaurs** (TEAR-uh-SORES, "Winged Lizards") or **Pterodactyls** (TEAR-uh-DAK-tils, "Winged Fingers"), these flying reptiles had leathery wings that stretched from their legs to an elongated forth finger on each hand. They came in many shapes and sizes, and often had strange-looking crests on their heads. Over 60 types of pterosaurs have been found. Some were tooth-less, while others possessed many sharp teeth in their beaks. Some had long tails; others were virtually tailless, and they could range in size from a small bird to a small airplane! Their fossils have been found on every continent except Antarc-tica. While not yet scientifically verified, modern sightings of pterodactyls have been reported in such places as Papua New Guinea, Indonesia, Africa and even the United States. This is not too surprising since they, along with all other land-dwelling creatures, were taken aboard Noah's ark and could have survived the great Flood!

# G is for GASTONIA

Ever heard of a dinosaur named Gastonia?
I knew it! I knew it! I knew it!
Gastonia had boney plates…and, oh, ah…
sharp spikes all over its "bod"—
the better to protect it from
your average "fallen" <u>theropod</u>.
So, now you know about Gastonia,
and I can say, "I told-e ya!"

A "theropod" is not a natural pea container but a two-legged dinosaur considered to be a meat eater.

**Gastonia** (gas-TONE-ee-UH) was a member of the ankylosaur (ang-KILE-uh-SORE, "Curved Lizard") family that is named after its discoverer, Robert Gaston. A heavily armored herbivore (plant-eating) dinosaur with short, sturdy legs that was 15-20 feet long and probably weighed 2-3 tons, it had hard, boney plates and sharp spikes all over its body. These defensive weapons protected *Gastonia* from theropod predators, such as tyrannosaurs, allosaurs and raptors, that likely became meat eaters after Adam's sin, when suffering and death entered our fallen world (GEN. 3). Prior to this, man and animals all ate plants. The most famous member of this family is *Ankylosaurus*, which could weigh up to five or six tons, be over 30 feet long and had a large, boney "club" on the end of its tail. *Gastonia* fossils have been found in Utah in the same bone bed as *Utahraptor*, which is much like the computer graphic velociraptors in the *Jurassic Park* films.

# H is for HADROSAUR

Hadrosaurs can quickly pad the sores
they get when roasting Hadro-smores,
but oft' grow sad about the snores
from their soundly napping Dad-rosaurs.
"Now, come on lads," says dear, ol' Dad,
"it's really not that rad a roar."
"Oh yes it is," insist the kids,
"in fact, it's all that bad and more!"

**Hadrosaurs** (HAD-ruh-SORES, "Sturdy Lizards"), also known as duck-billed dinosaurs, were the first species of dinosaur identified in America and one of the most common to roam the world. Teeth of this animal were originally found in the USA in 1855 and many of their bones— including some rare, very complete skeletons—have been found since then. The many varieties of this creature are divided into two sub-groups: Lambeosaurs, which have crests on their heads, and Hadrosaurs, which don't. A recent, nearly complete specimen from North Dakota named "Dakota" was extremely well preserved, containing not only fossilized bones but also skin, tendons, ligaments and even some of its internal organs! Such amazing preservation indicates that this dinosaur's burial and fossilization occurred very rapidly, such as in a catastrophic event like Noah's flood, and not gradually over millions of years as evolution says. Hadrosaur bones are found in the USA, Canada, Europe and Asia.

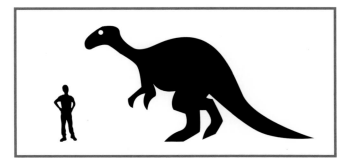

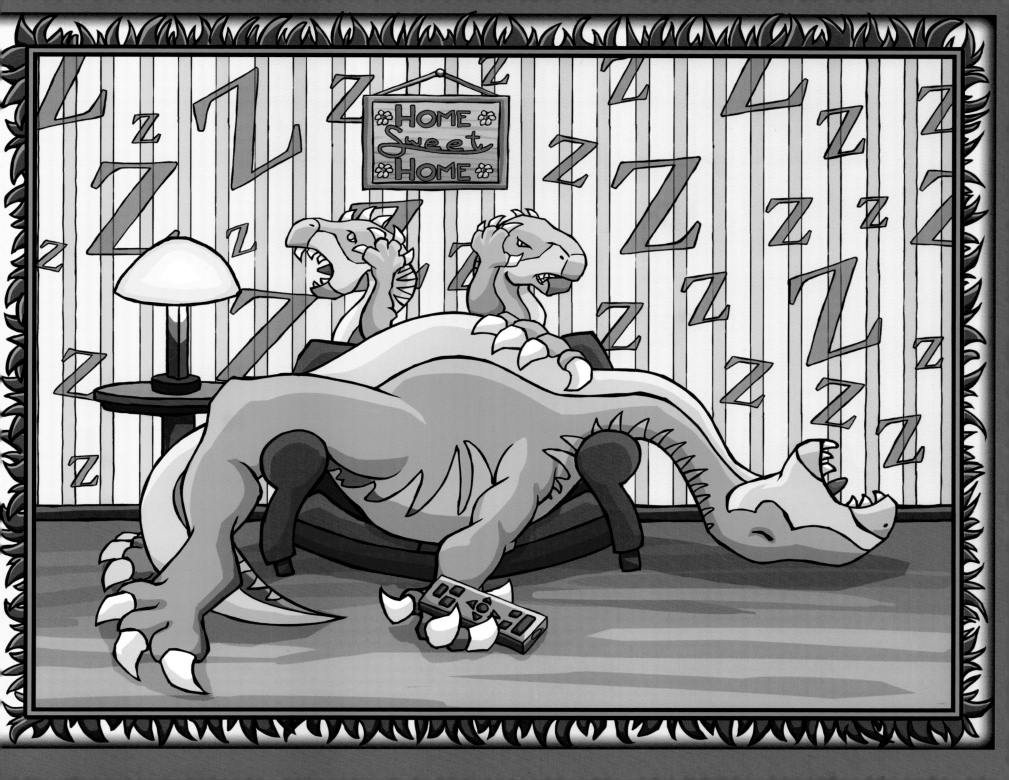

# I is for IGUANODON

The Iguanodon was not a con, nor did it tell a lie;
it simply had a horn that was lower than t'was high.
Turns out it didn't have a head horn
but a big spike for a thumb,
which may sound silly, weird or funny—
or even kinda dumb!
But with such sharp thumbs, an Iguanodon
might just want to mow your lawn!

**Iguanodon** (ig-WAHN-uh-DON, "Iguana Tooth") was one of the first dinosaurs ever discovered back in the early 1820s. It got its name from the fact that its teeth resemble those of an iguana, only much larger. It was a bipedal herbivore that sometimes walked on all fours. It grew to over 30 feet long and could weigh three to four tons. Instead of thumbs, it had sharp, boney "thumb-spikes," which it may have used to defend itself. Englishman Gideon Mantell, whose wife first discovered the bones, originally thought the spike was a horn on Iguanodon's nose until further discoveries revealed that it belonged to its hand. In 1878 the bones of at least 38 of these dinosaurs were excavated from a coal mine in Belgium—yet another example of a mass dino "graveyard." This one strongly indicates a watery catastrophe that included tons of vegetation, which is the material of which coal is made. In addition to Europe, hadrosaur bones are found in Asia, Africa and North America.

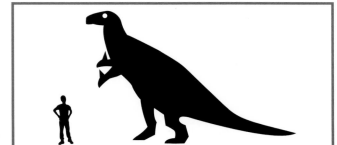

# J is for JAXARTOSAURUS

The Jaxartosaurus could wax cars, or ignore us,
or grow flax in a cart or sing in a chorus.
With a high, rounded crest on its big, duck-like gourd,
was "Jax," as some call him, a true hadrosaur?
Well, of course, don't you know, just believe what they say,
never mind how few bones have been found, by the way.
So relax, send a fax—but until then or before—
just don't ever play jacks with a jaxartosaur!

**Jaxartosaurus** (jax-AR-tuh-SORE-us, "Jaxartes Lizard") is believed to have been a type of hadrosaur that had a "helmet-like" crest on its head, based on a few bones found near the Jaxartes River in Kazakhstan, and in Russia and China. If it were a hadrosaur it would have been a bi-pedal herbivore similar in size to others of that family, standing up to 16 feet high and measuring up to 30 feet long. Its mouth would have contained a battery of hundreds of flat teeth to chew its diet of plant material. However, whether *Jaxartosaurus* actually is a separate species is doubtful because, as is true for much of evolution, proof for it is based only on fragmentary evidence and not on substantial facts. Like the existence of *Jaxartosaurus*, the belief that life evolved out of dead matter is based on even less evidence in the fossil record—like none! It actually takes more faith to believe a story like that than it takes to believe that a loving God created everything by His great wisdom and power, that man's sin brought struggle and death (Darwin's "war of nature") into the world, and that Jesus conquered sin and death to bring us new life, just as the Bible says.

# K is for KRONOSAURUS

"Oh, no, Doris, it's a Kronosaurus!"
someone yelled, as she swam in the Outback Sea.
But the huge marine reptile just grew a big reptilian smile,
as he spied Doris attempting to flee.
"Where's your mojo?" asked the hungry Krono.
Replied the terrified Dory, "I don't know.
Just don't eat me!"

**Kronosaurus** (CROW-no-SORE-us, "Kronos's Lizard"—named after the mythical Greek god, Chronos) was a large, short-necked pliosaur with four flippers, a short tail and a huge head that was about one-fourth the length of its body. Considered a ferocious, predatory marine reptile, it lived in the sea and breathed air like a whale, grew to over 30 feet long and had big, conical teeth, thought to crush the shells of some of its favorite prey—ammonites and turtles. However, as a top predator, it probably also ate fish and other marine reptiles, even the long-necked plesiosaurs! Pliosaurs, like *Kronosaurus*, and plesiosaurs would be terrifying creatures to encounter in the ocean. While evolutionists claim these creatures lived over 65 million years ago in the Cretaceous seas, they resemble the "sea serpents" mentioned in our (roughly) 3,500-year-old Bible (see letter L) far better than whales or sharks. In fact, museums kept fossils of marine reptiles in boxes labeled "sea serpents" into the 1800s, and sightings of sea serpents, such as the Loch Ness Monster, continue to be reported today. Could such fearsome creatures still exist? Fossils of kronosaurs have been found in the "Outback" of central Australia and in Columbia.

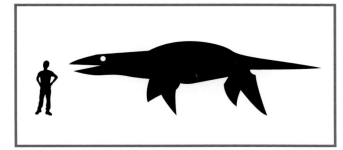

# L is for LEVIATHAN

Let's take a good look at Leviathan,
which the Bible mentions in Job 41.
Could this great beast have been a mere crocodile
or was it a fire-breathing dragon, though not so in style?
God said catching this thing would have been rather dire,
since apparently it could breathe out brimstone and fire!
So, is calling them crocs a "crock" or what,
or did real, live dragons once dwell on the earth?

**Leviathan** (Le-VIE-uh-THON, from a Hebrew word meaning, "twisted" or "coiled.") The Bible describes the Leviathan as a gigantic sea serpent or sea monster (PSALM 104:25-26). ISAIAH 27:1 refers to it as a "winding," "twisted" and "coiled" sea serpent and reptile. PSALM 74:14 indicates that some may have had multiple heads. In JOB 41, God asked Job questions about Leviathan—a creature he clearly knew—that no man could fish out of the water or prevail against. It had "terrible teeth," rows of sharp scales, and breathed smoke out of its nostrils and fire out of its mouth! While the end of the chapter indicates this beast also serves a symbol for Satan (called "that old serpent" and the "great dragon" in the book of Revelation), it was clearly a real, recognizable and terrifyingly large snake-like, meat-eating, fire-breathing reptile that lived in the sea in Job's time. That was just a few thousand years ago! Is it just a coincidence that almost every people group on earth has stories about dragons—some of which even breathe fire?

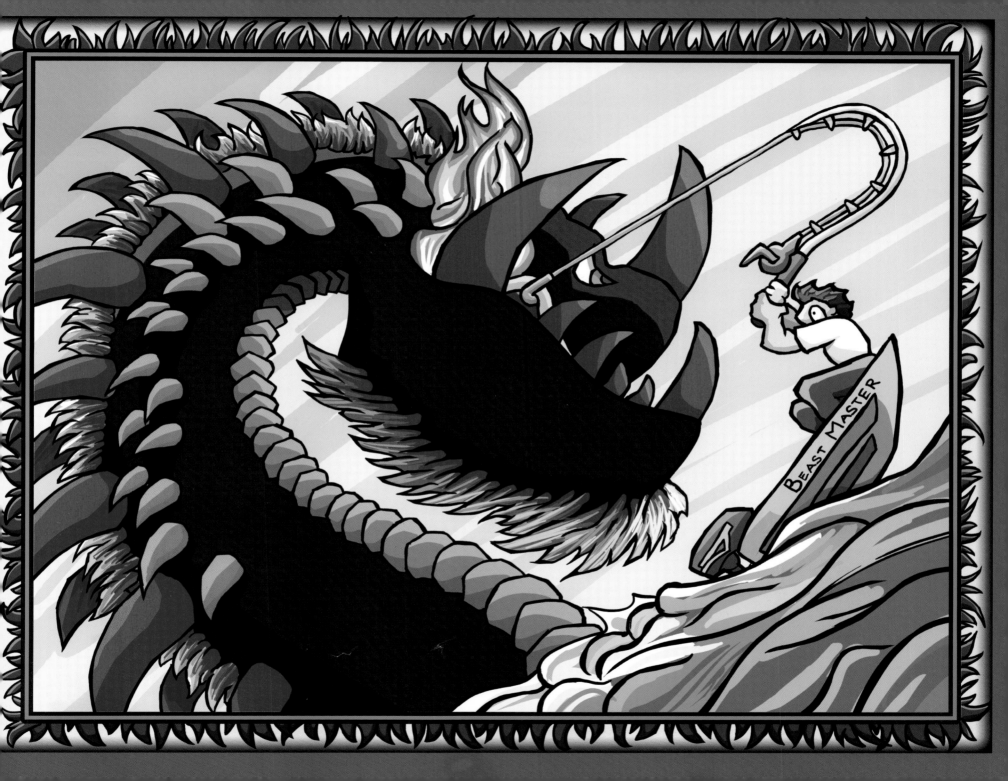

# M is for MONOCLONIUS

The head of Monoclonius was,
indeed, rather "boneous."
With a frill like a Triceratops,
it had just one big horn on its…"nose-ious."
It's said that these dinos really didn't miss touch—
which is good, cuz with "mono" they couldn't, well…kiss much!
Neither a clone, nor a stone, but possibly erroneous,
is the single-horned dinosaur named Monoclonius.

"Mono" is short for Mononucleosis, aka "the kissing disease". (+ makes people very tired and is spread through that yucky kind of boy-girl kissing.

**Monoclonius** (MON-uh-KLONE-ee-US, "Single Stem"—referring to its single-rooted teeth) was one of the first dinosaurs discovered in the United States. Edward Drinker Cope excavated it in Montana in 1876 near the site of Custer's Last Stand at the Little Big Horn. A relatively small member of the ceratopsian family, *Monoclonius* was a plant-eating dinosaur with a parrot-like beak and a bulky, tank-like body that reached a length of 16-20 feet, a height of nine feet and a weight of nearly 5,000 pounds. It had a large, boney frill on its head, but only possessed one main horn on its nose. Some believe that *Monoclonius* should be classified with a similar species of ceratopsians known as *Centrosaurus*. Fossils of up to 38 centrosaurs have been found in a mass bone bed in Alberta, Canada, which the scientists say was likely caused by "a flood." Imagine that! *Monoclonius* bones have also been found in Alberta.

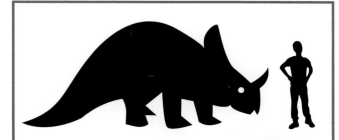

# N is for NANOTYRANNUS

Nanotyrannus would easily "tan" us,
that is, our hides—that is, could they scan us.
A juvey T.rex, or maybe not, as some say,
"Nano" was clearly a tyranno, either way.
While he may have dreamed of being as big as a bus,
if he wasn't a Rex that wouldn't mean very much.
When all's said and done, it may take a genius
to tell whether Nanotyrannus is a separate genus.

**Nanotyrannus** (NAN-uh-tie-RAN-us, "Tiny or Dwarf Tyrant") is either a smaller type of tyrannosaur or a juvenile *Tyrannosaurus rex*. Based on two small skulls about 22-inches long and another more complete skeleton, it is estimated that *Nanotyrannus* was only about 20 feet in length—about half that of *T.rex*. It also had more teeth, which were more knife-like than those of *T.rex*, was much lighter in weight and had longer leg bones than *T.rex*. This indicates that it could run faster than *T.rex*, or perhaps up to 30 miles per hour. Scientists are still undecided about whether *Nanotyrannus* is a separate species or merely a young *T.rex*. Considered by some a "primitive" tyrannosaur, its bones have been found in the same sediments as *T.rex*—the Hell Creek and Lance Creek formations—indicating that it did not live before *T.rex* but at the same time. In other words, whatever it is, *Nanotyrannus* did not evolve into *Tyrannosaurus*!

# O is for OTHNIELIA

Othnielia was a small, "bird-hipped" dinosaur
that walked on two feet.
It might have made a good pet cuz it didn't eat meat.
Given its name for a guy known as Othniel,
you could say that this dino wasn't named awful well.
But that didn't matter to little Othnielia,
for, you see, he was truly, very…oh…speedia
(fast, quick, swift…).

**Othnielia** (oth-NEE-lee-UH) was a small, plant-eating, bipedal dinosaur that was 4 to 6 feet long and weighed around 50 pounds. It was named after the 19th century American paleontologist Othniel Charles Marsh. *Othnielia* had a small head with large eyes, five fingers on its hands and four toes on its feet (all with claws), a stiff tail, short arms and long legs. Its shin bones were especially long, which likely made it a very fast runner, and speed was probably its only real defense against predators. With the average dinosaur being about the size of a large dog, *Othnielia* was probably near the size of the typical dinosaur Noah took on the Ark, along with young members of the larger species. Fossils of *Othnielia* have been found in Utah, Colorado and Wyoming.

# P is for PLESIOSAURS

Plesiosaurs could be sneezy old bores;
they had long necks and swam in the sea.
Otherwise known as "oceany" lizards,
some even carried smooth stones in their gizzards
that helped them grind food—but were no help in blizzards!
Whatever you think of them, this you can't ignore:
it would be hard to please,
much less squeeze or unease, a plesiosaur.

**Plesiosaurs** (PLEEZ-ee-uh-SORES, "Near Lizards") were marine reptiles with large bodies, short tails, four flippers and small heads that were thought to be carnivorous. While some had short necks, the classic *Plesiosaurus* had a long, snake-like neck that could reach to over half of their length, which could be up to 60 feet! Their fossils have been found on every continent—some along with small stomach stones or gastroliths, which they may have used to grind up their food or to regulate their depth as they swam in the ocean. There have been many reports of plesiosaur sightings in modern times, like the Loch Ness Monster in Scotland; however, none as yet has been scientifically verified. Nonetheless, it's entirely possible that some survived Noah's flood and may still be living today.

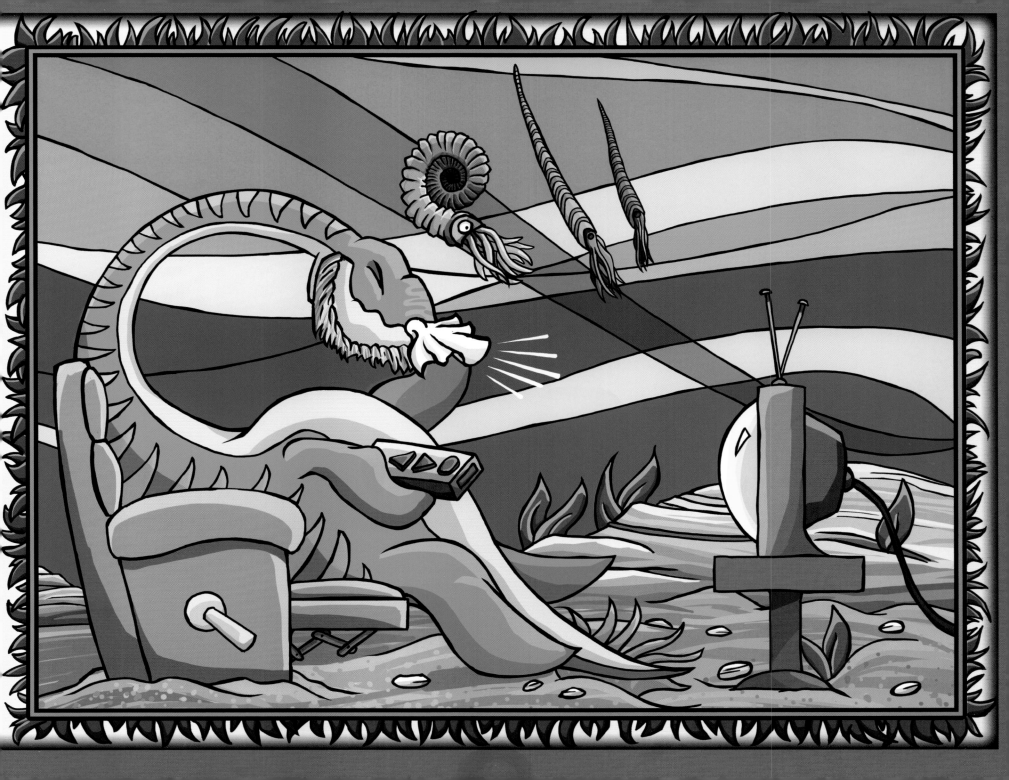

# Q is for QUETZALCOATLUS

The Quetzalcoatlus did not need an atlas
to soar through the skies of Denver or Dallas.
Big, lizardy flyers—sorta' like a living airbus—
why, some were undoubtedly even named Gus!
Found down in ol' Texas was Quetzalcoatl,
though few drove a Lexus or raised any cattle,
which is all just as well (one could say, "fiddle-faddle"),
cuz I doubt very many could ride in a saddle!

**Quetzalcoatlus** (KET-zahl-koh-AT-lus) was a giant pterosaur the size of a small airplane, with a wingspan that may have reached to over 40 feet! Named after the mythological Aztec feathered-serpent-god *Quetzalcoatl*, this flying reptile may have been the largest airborne animal that has ever lived. It had a large head with a bony crest and a long, toothless beak like a stork, and probably fed on fish, amphibians, lizards and maybe even on small or baby dinosaurs! Bones of *Quetzalcoatlus* have been found primarily in Texas. Many American Indian tribes have vivid stories of "thunder birds" with "bat-like" wings, which resemble pterosaurs like *Quetzalcoatlus* far better than any other flying creature, indicating that they may have existed in fairly recent times—and, indeed, may still exist.

# R is for RAPTORS

It's thought that raptors lived in "chapters"
and, though they weren't species adaptors
(as the evolutionists like to say),
they're known for many factors gathered 'long the way.
Fast and nimble, they had a "sickle"—
not a thimble—on their two (bipedal) feet,
all the better to shred their dinners,
since, after Sin, they did eat meat!

**Raptor** is the common name for a group of theropod dinosaurs known as **Dromaeosaurs** (DRO-me-uh-SORES, "Swift Lizards"). They were fast-running bipeds that had a large, sickle-like claw on both feet that they probably used to kill their prey after the Fall, along with a mouthful of sharp teeth. Whether based more on Hollywood or science, some claim raptors were quite intelligent and hunted in packs, coordinating their actions like wolves. This group includes *Velociraptor*, only 5-6 feet long and 2-3 feet tall (they were greatly exaggerated in *Jurassic Park*!), *Deinonychus*, 9-10 feet long and *Utahraptor*, reaching to over 20 feet in length. *Deinonychus* teeth have been dug up with ceratopsian bones by creationist bone diggers in Montana, indicating that they likely scavenged—or even preyed upon—dinosaurs like *Triceratops*! Along with North America, raptor fossils have also been found and South America and Asia.

# S is for STEGOSAURUS

A Stegosaurus once sang in a chorus
with our sweet, little gal, known as "Dory" or Doris.
With a brain the size of a walnut,
he fell in love with her—you say, "What?!"
Yes, he fell in love with our girl Dory,
but that's not the end of this silly story.
Dory, now older and much Stego-wiser,
will—ouch!—gladly warn you about thagomizers!

**Stegosaurus** (STEG-uh-SORE-us, "Roof Lizard") was a quadrupedal (four-footed) herbivore known for the large, pointed plates that ran along its back. The biggest of the stegosaur kind, *Stegosaurus* could grow to almost 30 feet long and 10-12 feet tall. It had a walnut-sized brain and a tail with four spikes called a **thagomizer**. Thagomizer spikes could be up to four feet long, making them quite useful for defense. Possibly also defensive weapons, its plates were probably used to regulate its body temperature like an elephant's ears. Fossils show no in-between stages linking stegosaurs to other dinosaurs, which is a serious problem for evolution. Even Darwin called the lack of "intermediate species" the "most serious objection" to his theory. Evolutionists must put their faith in "missing links" that remain missing, while creationists can accept the evidence as found: stegosaurs are stegosaurs, just as God made them. "Steg" fossils have been found in North America, Europe, India, Africa and China.

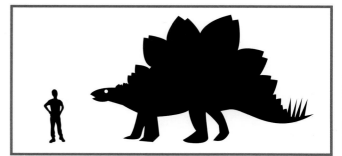

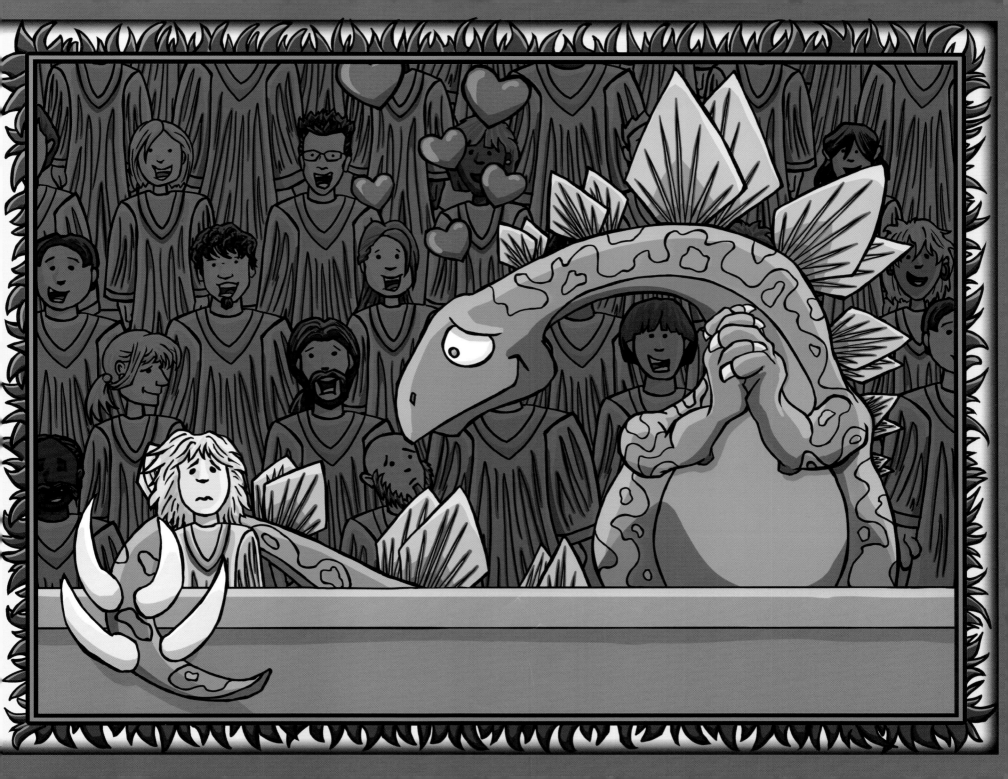

# T is for TYRANNOSAURUS REX

**Tyrannosaurus rexes love to scratch
and make their X's
on the backs, and legs and "neckses"
of less toothful dinosaurs.
In their bones _soft tissues_ have been found,
which shows it hasn't been all that long
since "Rex" has been around!**

*"Soft tissue" is not something you blow your nose with, but unfossilized organic material, like original blood vessels and red blood cells.*

**Tyrannosaurus rex** (tye-Ran-uh-Sore-us REX, "Tyrant Lizard King") was one of the largest and most fearsome-looking land animals ever created, growing to nearly 45 feet long, standing up to 13 feet tall at the hips and weighing seven or eight tons. Remember, *T.rex* was not created as a carnivore, but became one after Sin, the Fall and Corruption through micro-mutations and behavioral changes. An adult *T.rex* possessed a massive skull containing a mouthful of sharp, "tent-stake"-like teeth 6-8 inches long. It had two legs (bi-pedal) and tiny arms for its size and hands with two claws. Although *T.rex* was once pictured standing upright, new studies suggest it walked with its tail held straight out and head down. Before Sin, they would have had great posture, teeth and jaws for ripping up and gulping down watermelons and pumpkins! After the Fall, they may have started eating dead animals (scaveng-ing), but could have become predators of animals like *Triceratops* and *Hadrosaurus*. Indeed, they probably could have eaten virtually anything they wanted! *T.rex* bones have been found in the western United States, Canada and Mongolia. Recently, soft tissues have been found in some of their bones, which means that they cannot be millions of years old but only thousands of years old, as the Bible indicates!

# U is for UINTATHERIUM

Uintatheres looked rather weird,
with knobby heads and big teeth like shears.
They show up in the fossil record
quite fast then disappear,
which is why it's hard to take a photo
with a living Uintathere.
In fact, you'll seldom see a Uintatherium
outside of a natural history museum.

**Uintatherium** (you-IN-tah-THEER-ee-um, "Uinta Beast or Mammal") was not a dinosaur, but a strange-looking, rhinoceros-like mammal with three pairs of boney knobs on its head. One of the plant-eating megafauna ("large animals"), like mammoths or mastodons, that supposedly "evolved" after the extinction of the dinosaurs, its teeth were more like a tapir's and its bones were more like an elephant's. *Unitatherium* could grow to over five feet high and 13 feet in length and weigh more than two tons. Males had downward-pointing, dagger-like incisor teeth or tusks in their upper jaws that could be nearly a foot long. Uni-tatheres appear suddenly and without intermediate or transitional forms in the fossil record, not gradually as Darwinian evolution says "new species" should, and they disappear just as fast. That's because they didn't evolve from some-thing else but were created on Day 6 like dinosaurs (GEN. 1:24-25)—and, sadly, like most of the dinosaurs that got off the Ark, they did not continue to survive in the post-Flood world. Like many of God's creatures, their existence contradicts and confounds evolution. *Unitatherium* bones have been found in late- and post-Flood sediments of Utah, Wyoming, Colorado, Nebraska and East Asia.

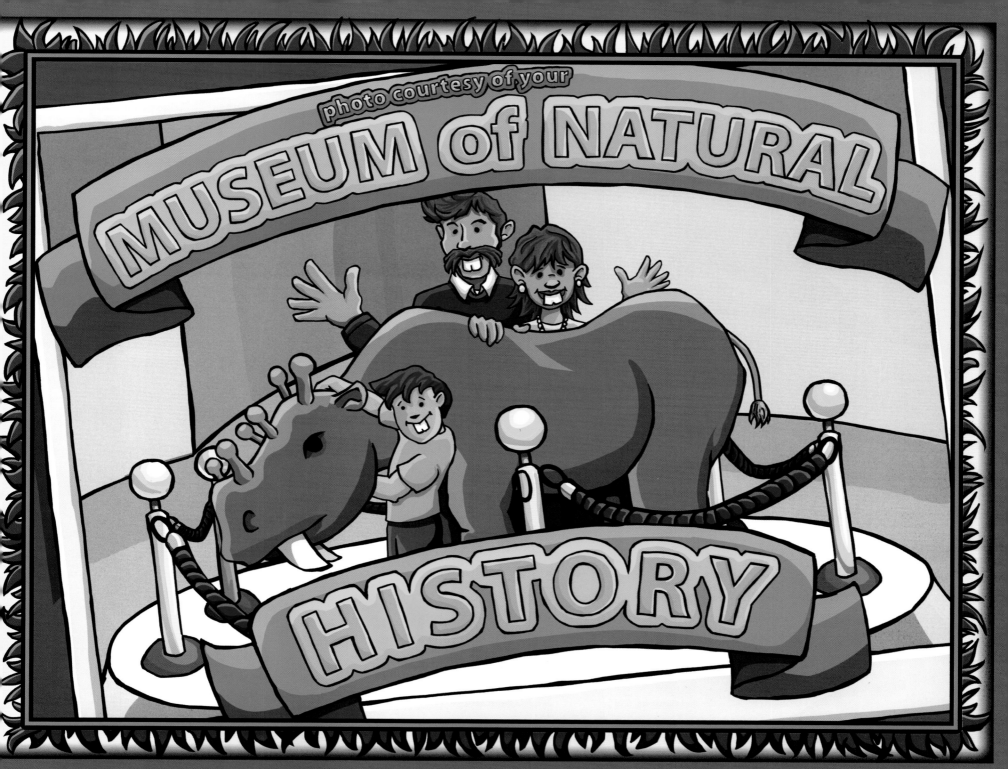

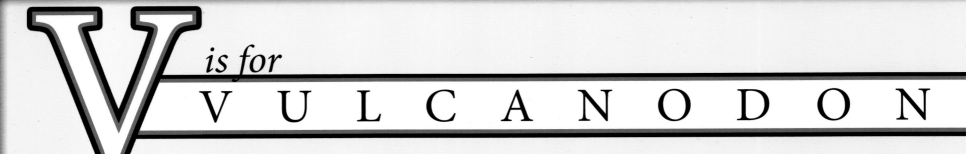

# V is for VULCANODON

Vulcanodon lived o'er and yon'
in Africa in times bygone (or maybe not!).
Thought to be an "early sauropod"
with sharp, "meat-eating" teeth,
it turns out that Vulcanodon would rather eat a wreath!
So, what can you say about Vulcanodon,
except that maybe it was named wrong?

**Vulcanodon** (vul-CAN-uh-DON, "Volcano Tooth") was a relatively small sauropod that was about 20 feet long and weighed four to five tons. It got its name from the fact that its fossils were found in sandstone between two layers of volcanic lava in Zimbabwe. Due to the sharp, knife-like teeth that were found with its bones, it was originally believed to be a "primitive sauropod" or prosauropod. However, those pointy teeth were later identified as belonging to a meat-eating theropod that probably fed on *Vulcanodon*. In other words, the teeth were used *on* not *by* Volcanodon, which turned out to be a meat-eater's meal, not its ancestor! So, rather than a "missing link," this dinosaur remains an unchanging member of the plant-eating sauropod "kind," just as God created it. Interestingly, reports of sightings of a small, living, *Vulcanodon*-like sauropod called Mokele-Mbembe have been coming out of central Africa for hundreds of years, but no Westerner has yet been able to produce solid evidence of seeing one. Maybe it will be you!

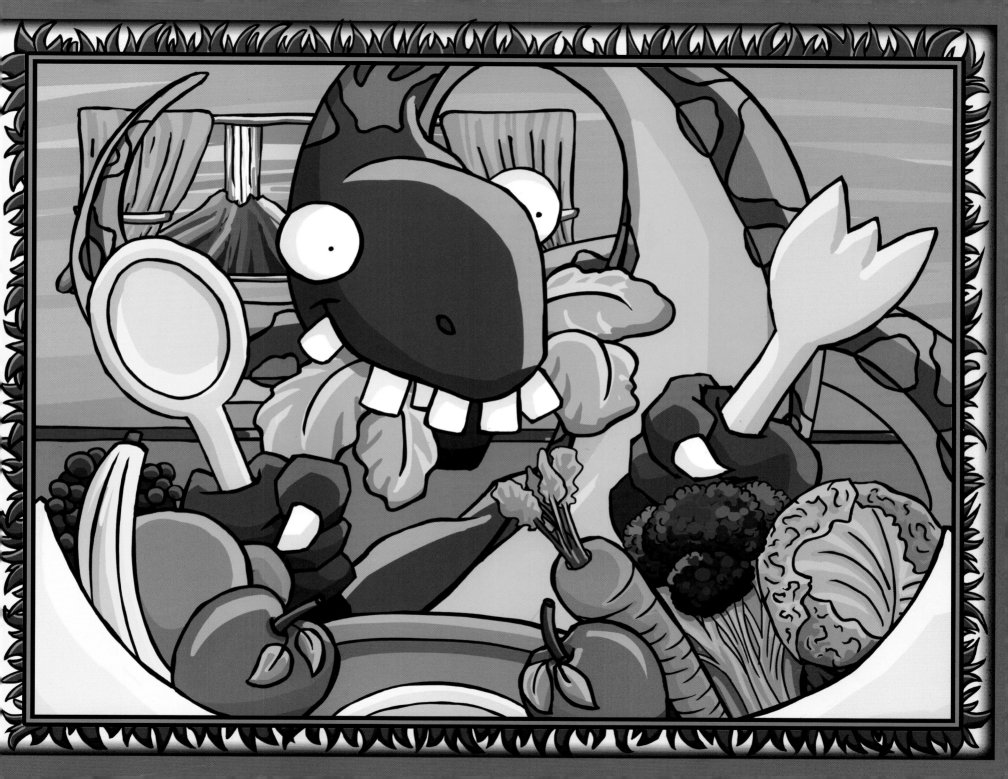

# W is for WOOLLY RHINO

Woolly Rhinos were not dinos;
they were woolly—that means mammal.
Nor could you say they were "enviros";
they thought global cooling was just fine-o.
While men hunted the Woolly Rhino,
if you tried to ride one this much we all know:
you'd have to be one silly Dodo!

*"Enviros" is short for environmentalists - people who believe that global warming or cooling is mainly caused by man. So, did the "Ice Age" result from men using spears to hunt woolly rhinos or fires to cook them?*

The **Woolly Rhino** was one of the megafauna ("giant animals")—like woolly mammoths—that lived during the so-called Ice Age or Pleistocene, the buildup of ice sheets that, at a maximum, covered about 30% of the continents around 500 years after Noah's flood. The Woolly Rhino could grow up to 12 feet long and six feet high, had a shaggy coat of hair and two horns on its face. Its nose horn could be up to three feet long! It lived in the cold climes of the northern hemisphere in Europe and Asia, ranging from England to Siberia in Russia. Cave paintings in France show pictures of Woolly Rhinos, indicating that they were hunted by men. This makes perfect biblical sense since both were created by God on the 6th day of creation (GEN. 1:24-27) around 6,000 years ago—and both survived the great Flood, which happened about 4,500 years ago, and was followed by a period of "global cooling," or, more correctly, polar cooling, which is called the Ice Age. However, during the "Ice Age," it was probably *warmer* than today in the more equatorial regions of the earth, which accounts for the big mammals, like Columbian mammoths and rhinos without wool, that lived in places like Florida.

# X is for XIPHACTINUS

The Xiphactinus was not, in fact, a bus,
but a giant fish from the Cre-ta-ceous.
It gobbled up other fish for lunch,
sometimes with or without au jus—
though at times it was had itself for brunch.
If you tried to catch a Xiphactinus,
you'd likely end up in a fuss
or even wind up in its guts!

**Xiphactinus** (Zih-FAC-tin-US, "Sword Ray") was one of the largest boney fish that ever lived. Reaching lengths of 15-20 feet, this giant, ocean-dwelling predator had a mouthful of sharp, needle-like teeth that could be three inches long. One fossilized skeleton found in Kansas contained the remains of another fish that was six feet long! This kind of perfect preservation of predator and prey is strong evidence for a sudden, catastrophic event (like a worldwide flood) that killed the eater and buried it— along with its "last supper"—in a very short time, not over thousands or millions of years. *Xiphactinus* was sometimes preyed upon by other sea creatures too, and its bones have been found inside a large, extinct shark. Commonly known as the "Bulldog Fish" due to its upturned mouth, *Xiphactinus* resembled a modern tarpon. Its fossils have been found in the United States, Europe and Australia.

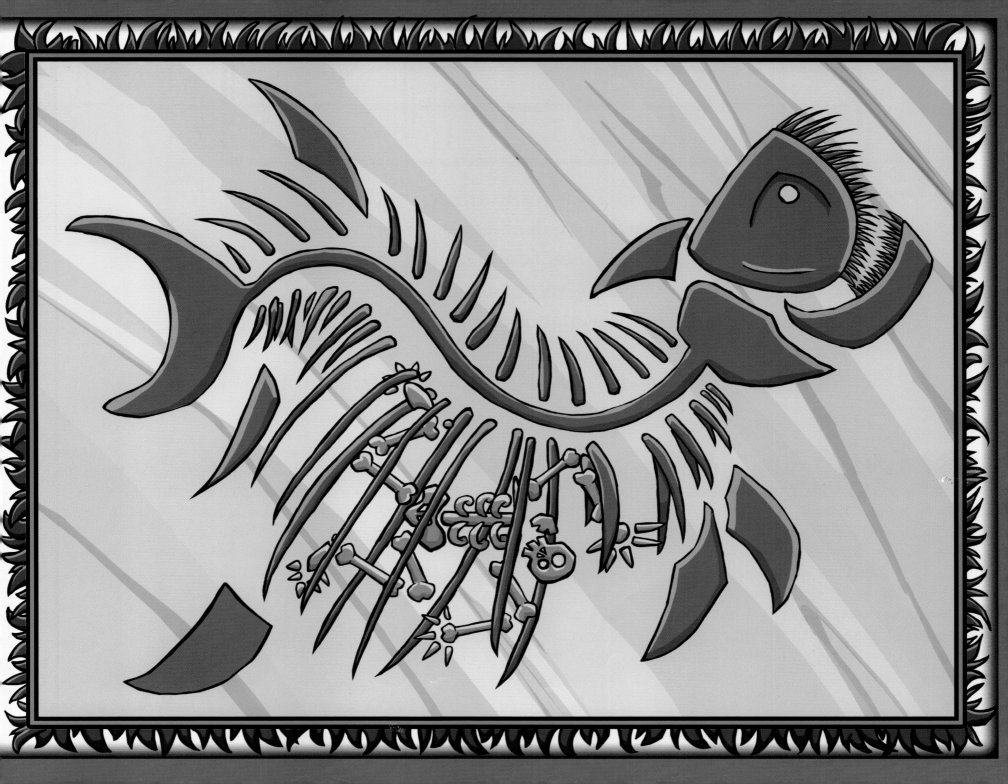

# Y is for YAVERLANDIA

Yaverlandia was really rather…uh, handy-ah.
Somewhat small and quite bone headed,
it was found on the Isle of Wight,
which is rather near Bri-tann-ia.
You see, Yaverlandy was probably a "Pachy"
—that is, a Pachycephalosaurus—
and "handy" cuz it would have had five fingers,
quite unlike a horse!

**Yaverlandia** (YA-ver-LAN-dee-AH, "from Yaverland") was a small, bi-pedal, plant-eating dinosaur whose only remains have been found on England's Isle of Wight. Named after fragmentary skull pieces found there on Yaverland Point, it was either the smallest member of the *Pachycephalosaurus* family or a juvenile, though some believe it was a meat-eating theropod. If it was a "Pachy," it would have had five fingers and a dome of bone on its head, though apparently Yaverlandia's skull had twinned frontal lobes. Like mountain sheep, males may have head-butted other males when competing for females and in self-defense. Other "bone-headed" creatures include human beings who deny the teachings of the Bible, which tells us that God created all living things during the six days of Creation Week (GEN. 1), or who ignore scientific facts, like finding soft tissues in dinosaur bones, which clearly shows that they cannot be millions of years old.

# Z is for ZYGORHIZA

A so-called "early" species with large and pointy teeth,
for a whale Zygorhiza
wasn't what you'd call a "biggy"—
and did not deliver pizza,
though they're sometimes known as "Ziggy."
While no one would despise ya,
no doubt it would surprise (or terrorize) ya
to have a Zygorhiza analyze ya!

**Zygorhiza** (ZIE-guh-RYE-za, "Yoke Root") is an extinct species of toothed whale. Like the killer whale, it had a sleek body, a narrow head and a mouthful of sharp teeth, which, after Sin, it probably used to eat small sharks, fish and squid. Relatively small, it was only about 20 feet long. Considered a "primitive" whale by some, *Zygorhiza* had a unique combination, or "mosaic," of interesting features shared by others of God's creatures. It had tiny rear flippers, used for mating in some whales, front flippers that were hinged at the elbow like a manatee's are and nostrils near the front of its nose, again like the manatee. In short, there was nothing primitive about it. Indeed, because, like the beluga whale, its seven neck vertebrae were not fused it had greater mobility and flexibility than most whales living today. Along with its larger "cousin" *Basilosaurus*, *Zygorhiza* is the state fossil of Mississippi, which is part of the "fossil whale belt" in the Southeastern United States. Commonly called "Ziggy," its fossils are also found in Florida, South Carolina and Georgia.

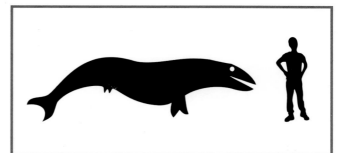

# Conclusion

In addition to what can be known about the behavior of fantastic animals from the past like the dinosaurs, the Bible also offers the best explanation for the geological record and the fossils it contains. Evolutionists claim that most of the rock layers on the earth, especially those containing fossils, were formed by the slow, gradual accumulation of sediments over vast periods of time (hundreds of millions of years). However, God's Word suggests that most of our planet's geological features were not formed by a vast amount of *time* but by a vast amount of *water*—namely, the worldwide flood of Noah (GENESIS 6-9). And Noah's flood was anything but a gradual, temperate event. It was God's judgment on the wickedness of mankind and the greatest cataclysm in the history of the earth!

While the Flood is often characterized by "40 days and nights" of rain (GEN. 8:12), the Bible also tells us that "all the fountains of the great deep were broken up" (GEN. 8:11). In other words, vast reservoirs of water and/or water in molten rock (magma) beneath the earth's crust were abruptly released—i.e., exploded onto the earth's surface. As rain pounded the world from dark, thundering skies above, picture massive earthquakes, gigantic geysers and great volcanic explosions erupting all over below, spewing water, fire, smoke, ash and rivers of steaming, red lava. This massive geological upheaval would have generated huge landslides, rockslides, mudslides and gigantic tsunamis washing over the planet and gobbling up everything in their path. In some places, as the subterranean water/magma reservoirs emptied, the earth's crust would have collapsed. Such global geologic violence would generate floodwaters rising over the highest land. As the biblical record of God's acts in history tells us: "...all the high hills under the whole heaven were covered....All in whose nostrils was the breath of the spirit of life, of all that was on the dry land, died....And the waters prevailed on the earth one hundred and fifty days" (GEN. 7:19, 22 & 24). And all of this was probably exacerbated by the violent separation of the continental plates, which likely created the continents as we know them today.

The rising floodwaters would have buried and fossilized creatures in a series of sedimentary rock layers circling the globe, beginning with the creatures that had the least chance of escape—those dwelling on the ocean floor and lacking mobility—the falsely so-called "simple" life forms like trilobites, clams, snails, sea stars, etc., etc. Then near-shore life forms would be buried, followed by lowland plants and animals. Finally, creatures from upland environments would be entombed. Land animals (and men) with greater mobility would have sought higher ground, inevitably only to suffer the same terrible fate.

Rather than a "gentle rain" falling on the earth until it produced "a flood," the flood of Noah was an *extremely* turbulent, *exceedingly* violent catastrophe, more like being tossed around in a mud-filled washing machine than sitting in a tub of rising bath water. No land-dwelling, air-breathing creature or man, could escape; it meant total doom and complete destruction to all—except for those securely enclosed in the Ark. Inside the walls of Noah's ark, which God had commanded faithful Noah to prepare, there was safety and peace. As the waters of Noah's flood subsided, mountains rose and valleys sank down at God's command (see PSALM 104:8), leaving behind layers of sediment with plants, dead animals and people turned into oil, coal and fossils. And, as the floodwaters ran off the still soft sediments, they sculpted most of earth's major geological features, leaving behind the amazing and beautiful geological/fossil record as a testimony to God's judgment of Sin. Once again, God's Word best explains God's world, encouraging us to trust His Word for the promise of salvation from Sin and new life found only in Jesus Christ. As the Bible also informs us, this same Jesus, Who died for our sins, rose from the grave and offers eternal life to all who believe in Him, is also our Creator:

*For by Him (Jesus) were all things created that are in heaven and that are on earth...All things were created through Him and for Him.*
COLOSSIANS 1:16

# Index of Creationist Fossil Groups

**FACT Dinosaur Digs (Montana)—Otis Kline**
**What:** Half-day, Full-day and Weeklong digs for T.rex, Triceratops, Hadrosaur, Thescelosaurus, Pachy, etc.
**Location:** Glendive, Montana
**Website:** www.creationtruth.org

**Baisch's Dinosaur Digs (Montana)—Shana Baisch**
**What:** "Take home dinosaur fossils, petrified wood, colorful rocks and precious memories from a day in the Eastern Montana badlands. Play paleontologist while you hunt for and excavate Triceratops, Edmontosaurus, and the elusive T.rex."
**Location:** Glendive, Montana
**Website:** www.dailydinosaurdigs.com

**Mt. Blanco Fossil Museum (Texas)—Joe Taylor**
**What:** Fossil evidence, sales, excavation, prep & casting
**Location:** Crosbyton, Texas.
**Website:** www.mtblanco.com

**Creation Studies Institute (Florida)—Dr. Tom DeRosa**
**What:** Ice Age Fossil Floats, finding fossils of mammoth, mastodon, armadillo, sloth, horse, shark teeth, etc. Also, weeklong dinosaur digs in Glendive, Montana, with FACT.
**Location:** Floats—Peace River, Arcadia, Florida
**Website:** www.creationstudies.org

**Creation Adventures Museum (Florida)—Dr. Gary Parker**
**What:** One-day Fossil Hunting Canoe Trips, Weekend Excursions and Weeklong "Creation Education Vacations," featuring hands-on workshops and vertebrate fossil collecting (mammoth, mastodon, giant armadillo, shark teeth, etc.) on the Peace River—by appointment only.
**Location:** Arcadia, Florida
**Website:** www.creationadventuresmuseum.org

**Creation Evidence Museum (Texas)—Dr. Carl Baugh**
**What:** July dinosaur and human footprint excavations on the Paluxy River.
**Location:** Glenrose, Texas
**Website:** www.creationevidence.org

**Answers in Genesis Creation Museum/Dinosaur Digs (Montana) —Buddy Davis**
**What:** Weeklong dinosaur digs in conjunction with FACT—T.rex, Triceratops, Hadrosaur, crocodile, turtle, etc.
**Location:** Glendive, Montana
**Website:** www.creationmuseum.org

**Adventure Safaris McGlenn Dinosaur Digs (South Dakota)—Russ McGlenn**
**What:** Dinosaur digs—Edmontosaurus, Hadrosaur, Triceratops.
**Location:** Lemmon, South Dakota
**Website:** www.tccsa.tc

**Southwestern Adventist University Dinosaur Project (Wyoming) —Dr. Art Chadwick**
**What:** Dinosaur bone—Triceratops, Hadrosaur, T.rex, etc.—excavation and taphonomic research.
**Location:** Hanson Research Station, Newcastle, Wyoming
**Website:** http://dinosaurproject.swau.edu

**Creation Science Association for Mid-America (Kansas/Missouri)—Tom Willis**
**What:** Family Creation Safaris to study geology, astronomy and fossils.
**Location:** Usually Kansas or Missouri
**Website:** www.csama.org

**Northwest Creation Network**
**What:** A good source of listings for creation adventures & field trips.
**Website:** www.nwcreation.net

**Creation Research (Australia)—Dr. John Mackay**
**What:** Fossil evidence and field trips.
**Location:** Queensland, Australia
**Website:** www.creationresearch.net

## Biography

**Terry P. Beh** is a professional writer and editor, who has worked primarily for Christian organizations for nearly 25 years. With a B.A. in English Literature and an M.A. in Professional Writing, his writing career began at Focus on the Family in 1988, where he became a Master Writer for ministry president James Dobson. In 1995 he joined the staff of Promise Keepers, where he worked in its Publications Dept. and then as Executive Writer for Bill McCartney. Since 2000 Terry has operated his own freelance writing business and currently operates Clouds of Light Publications, a book publishing company. His writing experience includes everything from books and feature articles to brochures, newsletters and fundraising letters to audio scripts, screenplays and poetry, and almost everything in between.

An avid outdoorsman and creationist, Terry's particular area of interest is paleontology (dinosaurs and fossils). Since 1999 he has participated in numerous creationist dinosaur digs and has served as a dig supervisor on many of them. In recent years he helped excavate two dinosaur skeletons in conjunction with the FACT creation ministry in Montana: a *Thescelosaurus* nearly 70% complete, and 50%-60% of a very large member of the ceratopsian family, which may be a new species. A number of his articles on dinosaurs and fossils have appeared in the Creation Research Society's newsletter, *Creation Matters*.

With a life-long love of dinosaurs, which started when he was six or seven years old, when he often mistakenly told people he wanted to be an "archeologist," Terry understands the fascination these creatures have for children and wants to use his God-given writing skills to turn kids away from evolution and toward our awesome Creator, Jesus Christ. Terry lives in Castle Rock, Colorado, with his wife Anne and children Christian and Amanda. He enjoys camping, hiking, rockhounding, fishing, outdoor photography and, of course, fossils.

For additional information on dinosaurs and fossils, for author interview requests and to order copies of *T is for T.rex*, please visit www.tisfortrex.com. Terry's publication company may be found at www.cloudsoflightpublications.com.

# Biography

**Daniel W. Sorensen** was amazed by the first mark he ever made with a pencil on paper and has never stopped. The wonder continued when he started mixing thick, colorful, messy paint and different colors emerged, which he found magical and opened up endless possibilities. Since then, he has discovered many other mediums, such as sculpture, printmaking and even digital artwork—for Dan there really isn't enough time in the world to create all the things he wants to.

Growing up in Lima, Ohio, Dan's parents always encouraged him to pursue his passions—even if that meant letting him believe that the *Brontosaurus*, that is, the *Apatosaurus*, which lived across the road in the woods was for real. The first movie he was allowed to stay up to watch was *Godzilla, King of the Monsters*. His seventh birthday included playing "pin the man in the dinosaur's mouth" and watching *The Valley of Gwanji*, a movie about cowboys and dinosaurs. Ever since, Dan's favorite books, movies and games have always contained elements of the fantastic. It was only natural that his debut book, *T is for T. Rex*, would be about something he's loved since he was a child!

After high school, Dan served as a submariner in the Navy. Subsequently, he received his B.F.A. from the Columbus College of Art and Design and moved from Ohio to Colorado, where he takes full advantage of its outdoor possibilities. Having worked as an artist/designer for "some pretty amazing" companies, in early 2012 Dan chose to pursue his lifelong dream to paint, draw, sculpt and create as a freelance artist, with subject matter ranging from realistic landscapes and people to whimsical creatures and monsters. He also strongly believes in using his God-given gifts for social justice issues, like human trafficking and Denver's homeless, as well as giving of his time and talent to his church.

This quote from Madeleine L'Engle's book, *Walking on Water: Reflections on Faith and Art*, pretty much sums it up for Dan, "The artist, if he is not to forget how to listen, must retain the vision which includes angels and dragons and unicorns, and all the lovely creatures which our world would put in a box marked 'Children Only!'"

Dan's fine art and illustrations can be found at www.dansorensen.com. His video and animations can be found at www.youtube.com/danzilla01.